THE
STATUE
OF LIBERTY

THE STATUE OF LIBERTY

MARY
VIRGINIA
FOX

JULIAN MESSNER
NEW YORK

The Lady casts a giant shadow.

Cover photo © Jake Rajs/Image Bank.

Color insert photo credits: National Park Service Photo, Richard Frear: pages 1, 2 and 7. Currier & Ives: page 3. National Park Service Photo, M. Woodbridge Willians: page 4. Laine Whitcomb: pages 5, 6 and 8.

Photo credits: New York State Department of Commerce: page 2. Laine Whitcomb: page 4. New York Convention and Visitors Bureau: pages 7 and 62. Library of Congress: pages 8, 9, 14, 15, 16, 17, 18, 20, 24, 30, 31, 32, 33, 39, 40 and 41. New York Public Library: pages 21, 22, 23, 24, 25, 26, 27, 28, 29, 34, 35, 36, 45, 48 and 52. Gerard Malanga, courtesy of New York City Parks Department: page 43. The Museum of Modern Art Film Stills Archive: page 49. National Parks Service: pages 55 and 59.

Library of Congress Cataloging in Publication Data

Fox, Mary Virginia.   The Statue of Liberty.

   Summary: Describes the planning, creation, history, and current renovation of the great statue in New York Harbor celebrating liberty.   1. Statue of Liberty (New York, N.Y.)—Juvenile literature. 2. Statue of Liberty National Monument (New York, N.Y.)—Juvenile literature. 3. New York (N.Y.)—Buildings, structures, etc.—Juvenile literature. [1. Statue of Liberty (New York, N.Y.) 2. National monuments. 3. Statues] I. Title.
F128.64.L6F69 1985   974.7'1   85-15421   ISBN 0-671-60482-1 (lib. bdg.)

1 2 3 4 5 6 7 8 9 10

INTRODUCTION

I n pictures, the Statue of Liberty is an impressive symbol of our heritage, but looking at her in person, standing on her twelve-story pedestal, her towering image is mind-boggling.

When Liberty was built one hundred years ago, no structure equaled her height. She once commanded New York City's skyline. Even now, as skyscrapers pass her mark, she is not dwarfed on her island home. She stands alone proudly, enlightening the world, protecting, it seems, the tiny humans who come to pay her homage.

The strong features of her face are not fixed in a smile, nor do they present a frown to the world at her feet. How could human hands have created such a statue? How could any artist visualize a monument on such a grand scale? What kind of mouth should balance a four-and-a-half-foot-long nose? Frederic Auguste Bartholdi took on the challenge.

The statue's mouth is three feet across. Her right arm rises forty-two feet above her shoulder. The length of her hand is 16½ feet. Even the size of a fingernail had to be planned in scale as thirteen inches by ten inches. Her left hand holds a tablet 23½ feet by 13½ feet, on which is inscribed the July 4 date of independence.

The copper used in the shell of the statue weighs one hundred tons. The weight of the steel skeleton is more than one hundred twenty-five tons. Liberty was built to last forever.

It was discovered only recently that Liberty was in need of restoration. Experts in two countries diagnosed her to be in a sad state of repair and have given her new life. The Statue of Liberty may prove as indestructible a monument as man or woman has been able to create. She is dedicated to our future as well as to our past.

LIBERTY'S BIRTH

The Lady, the Goddess, Miss Liberty—she's been called many names, but she has always been the symbol of freedom. She stands for the lofty ideals of our government at its best. She's George Washington, Abraham Lincoln, and apple pie all rolled into one.

When travelers arrive in New York City by boat or fly over it in a plane, the first object they see is the Statue of Liberty. She stands proudly, as if by her stern, formidable presence she is beckoning to those who are returning and welcoming those arriving.

There's a burst of patriotic pride. Shoulders straighten. Hearts beat a bit faster. No other art object calls forth the emotional attachment we feel for this 225-ton, 305-foot gallant lady. She elicits the same excitement as the "Star-Spangled Banner," fireworks, a marching band.

It's hard to remember that Americans didn't invent her, and at one time were even reluctant to accept her. She was a gift from the French people who looked across the Atlantic Ocean and liked what they saw. Democracy seemed to be working well. After less than one hundred years, the experiment in self-government was a success. Although there had been a civil war in the United States, the country had survived it, was stronger than ever, and was fast becoming a world power.

France's history had been filled with chapter after chapter of oppression in different forms, war and rebellion under various banners. The French were ready for democracy, but afraid of socialism. They wanted liberty, but with strict discipline. They expected peace, but at the same time glory. It was a hard list of requirements to satisfy. With Napoleon III in power, change without revolution seemed impossible. Still, many intellectuals of the day hoped to set up a foundation for change.

Édouard [René Lefebrve] de Laboulaye was one of these men. As a well-known lawyer, professor, and historian, he spent most of his time trying to influence members of the court to write a new constitution. This document would give power to elected officials and would put France back on a sound financial footing.

Frédéric Auguste Bartholdi, the sculptor who would eventually create the statue, was a guest of Laboulaye's at a dinner party in 1865. During the evening the conversation turned to the topic of gratitude between nations.

Some people felt it didn't exist. The relationship between France and Italy was given as an example.

France had helped liberate northern Italy from Austrian rule, but France had also kept troops in Rome. This had infuriated the Italians. Laboulaye conceded the point that no love was lost between France and Italy, then pointed out that in the United States of America, the names of Lafayette, Rochambeau, and de Grasse were honored. These Frenchmen had fought for American independence against the British during the American Revolution. Here was a fine example of France giving help and that help being appreciated.

Laboulaye reminded his guests that in little more than a decade the United States would be celebrating its one hundredth anniversary. What better way to solidify the friendship between the two countries than to design a monument that would be built by the united efforts of both nations? It would be a monument to American independence, one that might also stir republican sentiment in France. To put it bluntly, the statue would be a reminder of a political debt when France needed a helping hand.

The idea was applauded, but no one took the initiative to organize such a project. With the unsettled situation in France, the backing of such a grandiose scheme was impractical at the moment. But the proposal was not forgotten. Bartholdi would remember.

However, at the age of thirty-one, the sculptor was more interested in earning his reputation in his own country than in actively pursuing this new idea. He already had an impressive following of sponsors. The great test of a French artist was the Salon, a yearly exhibit of works of art in Paris. There was fierce competition. Only the most popular, noncontroversial works were chosen.

Bartholdi was nineteen years old when a marble statuary group of his was exhibited. Two years later his larger-than-life-size statue of General Rapp was placed in a position of honor in front of the building on the Champs Élysées during the opening of the Salon.

Bartholdi was never considered an innovative artist. He was a conformist, but his heroic statues appealed to the romantic taste of the day. Glorified monuments were popular. His circle of influential friends was growing.

The sculptor's ideas for gigantic statuary were first inspired by a trip to Egypt. He found monuments there that overshadowed anything seen in Europe. This was what Bartholdi wanted to create.

France was well represented in Egypt at that time. Ferdinand de Lesseps was in charge of the engineering of the Suez Canal, which was under construction. This impressive connecting link between Europe and the Middle East took ten years to build.

Bartholdi envisioned creating a great lighthouse at the entrance to the canal. It would be in the form of a female draped in a Roman toga.

He presented sketches to the Egyptian ruler, Ismail Pasha. The proposed statue closely resembled what is now so familiar to the world as the Statue of Liberty, but the Pasha had ideas of his own. Instead of a torch, he insisted the light should be carried on top of the statue's head, the way the local women carried jugs of water on their heads. Bartholdi agreed to go back to his studio in Paris and work on a new model.

On his way home he made a special trip to the shores of Lake Maggiore in Italy. He wanted to see a statue of Saint Charles Borromeo, at that time one of the largest statues in the world. It was also the first known example of a statue made of copper repoussé. This is thin sheets of metal worked with a hammer inside and out and supported with iron beams. This seemed to be the ideal method to use in constructing the lighthouse.

In the meantime, the Pasha had had second thoughts. There were better ways to spend his money. Bartholdi's statue was seen as a symbol of another culture standing guard over Egyptian territory. The project was cancelled. Bartholdi was very disappointed. He sent letters to everyone he had met in Egypt to try to save the project. It was no use.

Back in Bartholdi's country, events were taking place that upset any thoughts of monument building. Napoleon III had again promised peace, but in 1870 when he was old and sick, he allowed himself to be trapped into a war with Prussia. Bismarck, the acting prime minister of Prussia, knew that his army was ready for combat. The French army was not. The Germans marched in and took over Paris.

Frédéric Auguste Bartholdi had never been a political man, but his patriotism was kindled. He volunteered his services at once. He served as aide-de-camp to General Garibaldi during the brief war.

The French army fell during the first few months of the war, the emperor with it. Laboulaye was finally to have his way. A republic was eventually formed to try to put together a stable government, but not before there had been much internal turmoil on top of a degrading defeat.

When the armistice was finally signed, the two French border provinces of Alsace and Lorraine were handed over to the Germans. Bartholdi had been born in the city of Colmar in the province of Alsace, as had his father and grandfather before him. Although he had been educated in Paris, he considered the family holdings in Colmar his home. That was where his roots were. His mother still lived there.

The loss of his homeland embittered Bartholdi. His thoughts turned more frequently to America. It was time to seek help from a friend. Perhaps the United States might be persuaded to use diplomatic pressure against the Prussians.

He didn't know how he'd do it, but he wanted more than ever to visit this free country for himself. He hadn't forgotten Laboulaye's suggestion of a friendship gift in the form of a monument. He needed a new commission. He could use this as an excuse to travel.

Bartholdi consulted with Laboulaye, who was pleased that someone had stepped forward to further the idea. Again they spoke of the hope that a monument could be sponsored as a joint effort. Laboulaye was not without friends across the Atlantic. He gave Bartholdi letters of introduction to several important families who might be interested in promoting the project.

Bartholdi may not have been the most talented artist of his day, but he was an excellent negotiator, diplomat, and persuader. He was not above flattery to further his goals. A rather dashing figure—dark hair, penetrating eyes, a clipped beard and mustache—he liked to wear a flowing tie to accentuate the artistic image he wished to project. He was the very model of a romantic hero of the nineteenth century.

The sculptor's mother was a great influence on her son. She would have preferred that he not leave her for his first trip to America, but that dream had been in his mind for too long to be disregarded. It was important, he explained to her, that he start a personal campaign for the monumental work he had been sketching on paper. Only if he could gain support of officials in America could the project become a reality. She consented, but made him promise to keep her informed of all his travels and meetings, a task he took care of almost daily.

Bartholdi first sighted America on June 21, 1871. He was one of the first on deck to view the shores of this, his idealized "sister country." What he initially saw excited him.

The skylines of New York, Brooklyn, and Jersey City blended together as if they were a stone wall. Bartholdi was pleased, he noted in a letter, that they had left a fringe of grass at the shore, which was welcome after his stay "in the realm of the fish."

His ship sailed through the narrow channel at the harbor mouth, past Bedloe's Island. A small garrison was still kept at Fort Wood on the island. The island had at one time been a haven for Tory sympathizers during the War for Independence. Before the war it had been a place for old-time sailing ships to dock for provisions before heading out on long sea voyages. "A commanding and protective site which all ships must pass," he noted.

From the very beginning, this was his first choice for the site of the statue. She should stand alone and be seen from land as well as water, Bartholdi believed.

The *Generale Transatlantique* docked at a North River pier. After going through customs, Bartholdi hired a carriage to take him to his hotel. His first impressions were recorded for his mother's benefit. He was surrounded by a milling of people in a hurry, he said, some neglected streets with potholes, street lamps of unequal heights, and displays of goods on

New York harbor, around 1885.

11

sidewalks as one might see at a country fair. He noticed that only the main streets were usually well kept and lined with tall houses. But with the eye of an artist, he complained that they were a hodgepodge of styles in bad taste.

Bartholdi seems to have had a slightly better impression of the people he met. Laboulaye's friends opened up an impressive series of introductions. Bartholdi soon found himself talking about the monument to Horace Greeley, publisher of the New York *Tribune*, and George William Curtis, the editor of *Harper's Weekly*.

His enthusiasm met with only mild support. He never mentioned how much this lavish gift would cost.

Bartholdi realized all too well that he needed wealthy backers. He had an interview with Cyrus Field, who had just put a cable under the Atlantic Ocean. This project had proved both useful and profitable. The profitability of a statue of liberty as a lighthouse was not all that obvious.

Bartholdi's stay in New York gave him an opportunity to renew his friendship with the family of John LaFarge, whom he had met in Paris. He accepted their invitation to spend time at their Newport, Rhode Island, home, a welcome change from the city. On this visit, he first met his future wife, but he was too busy at that time to pursue a courtship.

The sculptor had obtained a letter of introduction to the president of the United States, Ulysses S. Grant. He was to meet the president at the summer White House in Long Branch, New Jersey. Bartholdi was amazed at the modest life-style of the president. The unpretentious two-story frame house was close to the ocean but "devoid of trees or any semblance of lawn," he wrote.

Later in July Bartholdi was able to go to Washington. There too, he found a lot to criticize. He felt the cupola of the Capitol building was imperfect. The Washington Monument, which was in the process of being built, was much too austere a work of art to suit Bartholdi's taste. "Much dust, much sun, much flies," he wrote of Washington.

It is a wonder the Statue of Liberty was ever completed as a gift to a country with so many shortcomings, but Bartholdi was not there to waste time. He headed west to see what more there was to the land of opportunity he'd dreamed of for so long.

He traveled by train to Niagara Falls, and from there to Chicago, which, he wrote, was the most American city he had seen. In 1804 Chicago had had five inhabitants; in 1871 there were 299,000, an enormous population running around pressed by the "stomach ache of business."

The grandeur of the Rocky Mountains matched Bartholdi's expectations. His descriptions were poetic: "red masses of rock extravagantly shaped; water falls cascading from the sky; even some diabolical sights as in fairy tales."

He stopped in Salt Lake City and met Brigham Young, the great Mormon leader and "the happy husband of sixteen wives and the father of forty-nine children." He was asked to paint Young's portrait, but declined, saying he had to see still more places. He was on his way to San Francisco.

Wherever he stopped, he tried to organize groups of people who might continue to work for the memorial monument after he was gone. But the farther he traveled from the proposed site of Liberty, the weaker the response. What most people felt—even if they didn't voice the sentiment—was that if New York wanted a lighthouse, New York should pay for it.

His own travel expenses came out of his personal funds. So that the trip would not be a total financial loss, he sought orders for his work from any source that presented itself. When he eventually headed back to France, he had received a commission for a sculptural frieze to decorate the Unitarian Church of Boston. He was returning home with seeds sown, but no crop yet to cultivate.

Bartholdi had also been corresponding with Laboulaye, giving his mentor a slightly more positive picture of the American attitude toward the monument than was the truth. Yet his hope and desire for a finished statue probably colored his convictions.

The reception he met on his return to his homeland was heartening. Laboulaye assured him funds would be available for the construction of the statue. They were both sure that when the Lady began to take shape, Americans would open their wallets and show their generosity. But first there had to be something to show them.

Bartholdi had been experimenting with different images. Just what did an abstract idea like freedom look like? At one time Bartholdi had envisioned America as a young man— proud, almost savage, his arms resting on a machine, a horn of plenty at his side. But those weren't exactly the qualities he wished to portray. The image of Columbia imprinted on American coins was a closer match to his ideas, but she was too remote, too placid, offering no hint of passion, inspiring no real emotion.

Bartholdi worked on a dozen small clay models. It was said he used his mother's strong profile for Liberty's face. The classic pose was to incorporate symbolic details: the broken chain of tyranny at her feet; the open book on which was inscribed the date of the country's independence; the seven points of her crown representing the seven continents and seven seas of the world; and the torch held high to enlighten the world of the freedom, liberty, and democracy of a strong nation.

Some critics said that these symbols were only additions to the rejected Suez Canal model. Bartholdi vehemently denied that he had reworked an older idea. This was a project fresh from his imagination, dedicated only to the United States and designed especially for Bedloe's Island, the place he had already selected as its site.

The model for the statue that most closely resembles the monument.

The final clay-into-plaster model, standing slightly more than four feet in height, was photographed for the papers. The actual project got under way in 1874 when a committee called the Union Franco-Americaine was founded to direct the fund raising. Laboulaye was named its president.

A year later a huge campaign was launched at a banquet in Paris. The model was shown on a pedestal beside the speakers' table. A painting of the proposed statue as it would appear shining at night in New York harbor was hung on the far wall. Glorious words were composed for the occasion. "We will declare by this imperishable memorial the friendship that the blood spilled by our fathers sealed of old between the two nations."

The actual construction of the statue took place in the cavernous workshop of Gaget, Gauthier and Company on Chazelle Street in Paris. Copper $3/32$ of an inch thick was the material chosen for the skin of the statue. A 9.4-foot working model, $1/16$ the final scale, was enlarged first to a plaster model $1/4$ size, then into manageable sections of the full-size statue.

With each transfer, hundreds of measurements were taken. From some three hundred main points on the second enlarged model, fine wires led to twelve hundred points on the huge sections that together would form the final statue. Around this copy carpenters fitted narrow pieces of lumber in latticed molds. These wooden mounts were strong enough to withstand the hammering of the metalworkers as they shaped the copper into sharp folds and fine contours.

Each stage found Bartholdi smoothing out wrinkles and simplifying lines. He kept constant watch on the mold builders and the copper beaters. He had many meetings with the finance committee.

At the same time, he worked on other pieces to pay his living expenses. He accepted a commission from Adolphe Thiers, president of the French Republic, to create a statue of Marquis de Lafayette to be placed in New York's Union Square and to be presented during the centennial year.

There was no chance now for Liberty to make her appointed birthday in 1876, although her right arm, carrying the torch, was rushed to completion so that it could be displayed during the festivities in Philadelphia. It was hoped this display would spur reluctant contributions from the United States. Bartholdi had read newspaper accounts that other American cities—Boston, Philadelphia, Milwaukee, and San Francisco—had offered to find a site for the monument if New Yorkers failed to come up with the funds for the pedestal. Bartholdi wanted to squelch any such change. He planned on making his second trip to New York during the centennial year. It was time to confer with the pedestal committee.

A part of the statue being constructed in the Paris workshop.

Bartholdi left as a bachelor and returned with a wife. Her name was Jeanne Emilie Baheux de Puysieux, a Frenchwoman who had lived in Canada for some time. She was devoted to Bartholdi and intensely proud of, as she called it, his genius. A friend of the LaFarge family, she had met the sculptor during the summer of 1871.

Soon after Liberty's arm was put on display, Bartholdi and his bride left for Paris where the rest of the work was progressing more smoothly. The torch was to remain in the United States until just before the final presentation ceremony. After the Philadelphia Centennial Exposition closed, the torch was to be exhibited in Madison Square in New York City. Twelve people could stand on the rim of the torch. There was a twenty-cent charge for the privilege.

Other fund-raising schemes were planned on both sides of the Atlantic. There were auctions and raffles, benefit theatrical performances, art and poetry contests, and door-to-door solicitation.

Bartholdi applied for a patent design of the statue. Already people were selling cheap, six-inch copies of Liberty and buttons with Bartholdi's image. The copies of Liberty were in direct competition with the small models that were cast in the workshop of Gaget, Gauthier and Company. Half of the profit from their sale was to go to Bartholdi and half to the building fund.

Bartholdi had chosen Eugène Viollet-le-Duc, a masonry engineer, to devise a way to prop the statue up and secure it to a base the Americans still promised to build. Viollet-le-Duc planned to keep the statue stable just by its own weight. She would be filled with sand, but sand in compartments so that if repairs were required, one section at a time could be emptied. The engineer died in 1879 before his inner honeycomb was constructed.

GUSTAVE EIFFEL

Fortunately, Bartholdi turned to a much more innovative and imaginative engineer to carry out the work. Alexandre Gustave Eiffel, forty-seven at the time, was the creator of an entirely new technique in bridge-building. He used great sweeping arches and tall iron pylons strengthened with filigreed girders.

Eiffel's plan for the statue consisted of four iron piers rising ninety-seven feet and held together by nine levels of horizontal struts and diagonal cross-bracing. A secondary framework of lighter iron trusswork, or belts, reached toward the statue's skin, following

Construction of the statue in Paris.

its shape but not quite touching it. The belts were connected to the skin through riveted copper saddles, with an insulating material to keep the two metals apart. It was known that the chemical reaction between the iron and copper would cause the metals to rust.

The toes of the statue.

The early construction of the left hand and arm. Notice how small the men appear next to the hand.

Drawing of the design of the pedestal by Richard M. Hunt.

The skeleton was to work as a network of tight springs holding the pieces firmly, yet allowing a slight play of motion when temperature and wind conditions caused the statue to shift. The weight of the copper sheeting was distributed evenly so that each part of the framework held up its proper share. The cross braces were attached to the central pylon every 12½ feet. This central core supported the outer shell. This was the forerunner of curtain-wall construction, later to be used to build modern skyscrapers.

In the United States, plans for the pedestal had been drawn up by the distinguished architect Richard M. Hunt. It was estimated that construction would take nine months and would cost more than the original estimate of $125,000.

Great plans had been proposed for the ceremonial dedication of the statue, but few funds had been collected to make that dedication possible. The one man who took up the challenge to "erase the embarrassing image of uncouth incivility of the Americans" was Joseph Pulitzer. In 1883 he had taken over the ownership of *The World,* a newspaper that had once belonged to Jay Gould. Pulitzer needed a good cause to put the waning newspaper back on its feet. Who could argue with the cause of liberty? It would give him a chance to attack the committee "of bumbling millionaires who had done nothing except give banquets to hear themselves talk."

On May 14, 1883, *The World* ran an editorial bound to win the approval of its mass readership. It criticized the millionaires of New York who spent fortunes on their own luxuries but haggled over the pittance needed to put Liberty on her feet—"Liberty, the symbol of equality of all citizens of the Republic." If these men of wealth were unwilling to spare the country humiliation, *The World* would take up the challenge. All donations of one dollar or more would be accepted and the donors' names would be listed in the paper.

Day after day pathetic letters were printed to show how even the poorest citizens were ready to sacrifice their last cent and a hot meal for the Liberty fund. Whether the letters were real or not, they were good copy.

Newspapers in New York during the spring and summer of 1885 ran articles about and advertisements for the pedestal fund.

The Copies of THE WORLD Printed and Sold on Sunday Last Aggregated

230,220.

The Average Circulation of THE SUNDAY WORLD is Larger than that of any other Newspaper Published on the Western Hemisphere.

The Copies of THE WORLD Printed and Sold on Sunday Last Aggregated

230,220.

The Average Circulation of THE SUNDAY WORLD is Larger than that of any other Newspaper Published on the Western Hemisphere.

The World.

NEW YORK, TUESDAY, AUGUST 11, 1885---WITH SUPPLEMENT.

PRICE TWO CENTS.

VOL. XXVI., NO. 8,757.

THE SPECTRE IN GRANADA.

A CONDITION MORE HORRIBLE THAN THAT OF NAPLES LAST YEAR.

MURDERED IN HIS HOME.

A WEALTHY BROOKLYNITE SHOT DOWN BY A HIDDEN FOE.

ONE HUNDRED THOUSAND DOLLARS!

TRIUMPHANT COMPLETION OF THE WORLD'S FUND FOR THE LIBERTY PEDESTAL.

Story of the Greatest Popular Subscription Ever Raised in America—How the Republic Was Saved from Leading Disgrace—An Event for Patriotic Citizens to Rejoice Over—A Roll of Honor Bearing the Names of 120,000 Generous Patriots—The Flags of France and the American Union Floating in Sisterly Sympathy—Over $5,300 Received Yesterday—The Grand Total Foots Up $102,006.39—A Generous Lady Pays $130 for the Washington Cent.

Back in Paris, the great statue was assembled outside the workshop studio. It towered over rooftops and caused traffic jams in the area as people flocked to see the giant lady. Édouard de Laboulaye, the originator of the grand project, did not live to see her standing so proud and tall. The position of president of the Union Franco-Americaine was taken over by Ferdinand de Lesseps, the French engineer responsible for the Suez Canal and now hoping for a try in Panama.

He was the official who made the formal presentation of the statue to Levi P. Morton, the American ambassador in Paris, on July 4, 1884.

The erection of scaffolding outside the Parisian workshop.

The head of Liberty on display in a Paris park in 1883.

The statue rose over the Paris neighborhood, waiting for transport to America.

24

The foundation being built for the pedestal.

The announcement that the French government had agreed to finance the transportation of the statue to America was greeted with enthusiasm and relief by the American committee. The gift was accepted, but it had no place to go. Construction of the pedestal had not even been started yet.

On August 5, 1884, the cornerstone of the pedestal was laid. A copper box with a variety of items of historical interest was enclosed in the hollow granite block. Among the items was a fifty-cent coin minted in 1824, the year Marquis de Lafayette visited the United States. The calling cards of the dignitaries present at the ceremony were a last minute addition to the copper box.

The cornerstone of the pedestal being laid in August, 1884.

The pedestal continued to grow, block upon block reinforced with concrete. At the time, it was the largest single concrete mass ever built. "Amerians could be proud not just of the base size but of its beauty," *The World* wrote. It was a masterpiece of design, fully complementing, without rivaling, the majesty of the statue that would rise above it. Liberty's final height of three hundred five feet would make her the tallest object in New York City.

Once more Bartholdi arrived in New York harbor to consult with chief engineer Major General Charles P. Stone in planning the final steps for mounting the statue.

Meanwhile Liberty had been taken apart. Two hundred twenty-eight cases were packed with the pieces of the delicate copper shell. A small ship, the *Isère,* had been cut out on her port side so the bulky crates could fit. During the two-week crossing, the ship sailed into some very rough weather. Water poured into her hold, and there was a time when the captain was afraid that Liberty might end up on the bottom of the Atlantic. However, she arrived in New York on June 17, 1885, amid great celebration and fanfare. The pedestal was still being built. It was completed in April 1886.

FRANK LESLIE'S
ILLUSTRATED
NEWSPAPER

Entered according to Act of Congress, in the year 1885, by Mrs. Frank Leslie, in the Office of the Librarian of Congress at Washington.—Entered at the Post Office, New York, N. Y., as Second-class Matter.

No. 1,553.—Vol. LX.]   NEW YORK—FOR THE WEEK ENDING JUNE 27, 1885.   [PRICE, 10 CENTS. $4.00 YEARLY. 13 WEEKS, $1.00.

The arrival of the French ship, Isère, *bearing the statue.*

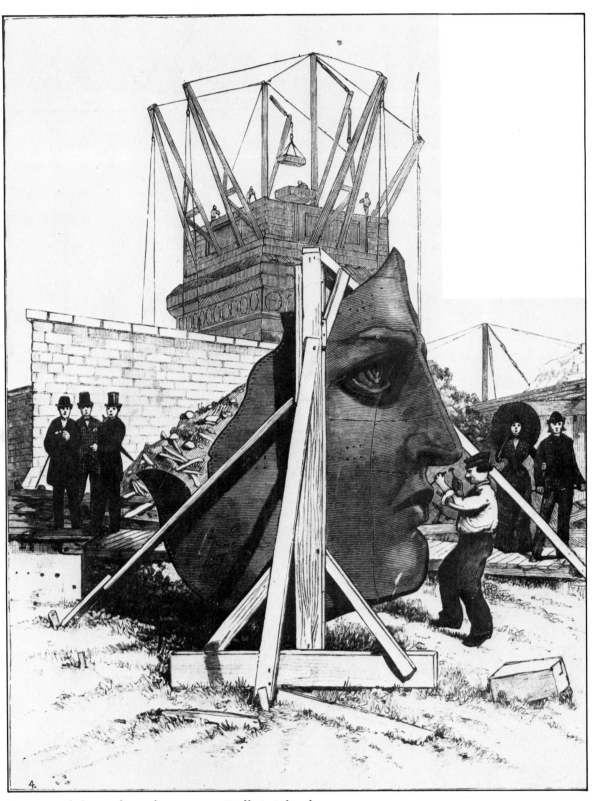

Progress of the work on the statue on Bedloe's Island.

Details of the statue's foot, face, crown, hand, and flame.

29

The pedestal completed and construction of the statue underway.

Liberty minus her face three weeks before the unveiling.

Putting in her face.

Elevation, plans, and a section of the pedestal showing how the statue was to be anchored.

It took another six months to mount the gigantic statue. Over three hundred thousand copper rivets held her skin together. The city of New York finally awoke to the magnitude of the gift it was about to receive. The dedication ceremony was to be a never-to-be-forgotten celebration. However, some of the unforgettable moments would have been better lost to history.

THE REPUBLIC OF WASHINGTON. — GREETING TO — THE REPUBLIC OF LAFAYETTE.

The World.

VIVE L'ENTENTE FRATERNELLE DES DEUX RÉPUBLIQUES.

VOL. XXVII., NO. 9,200.   12 PAGES.   NEW YORK, THURSDAY, OCTOBER 28, 1886.   12 PAGES.   PRICE TWO CENTS.

HERR MOST LIKES GEORGE.

THE CONVICT SAYS THE LABOR MOVEMENT WILL LEAD TO SOCIALISM.

WAR ABOUT BOSTON.

IT WAS PRIVATE WINE

DIMENSIONS OF THE STATUE.

FIGHTING FOR A BRIDE.

Shipwreck on the New Jersey Coast.

McClellan's Small Dictator.

Failure of a St. Louis Drug House.

Fatal Fire in Virginia.

Armor-Workers' Wages Advanced.

Vogal Brothers,

LIBERTY'S STORY.

Significance of France's Gift to the American Republic.

How the Grand and Colossal Statue was Conceived.

The Artist Bartholdi's Masterpiece from Birth to Dedication.

History of the Pedestal and "The World's" Part in Its Erection.

The Glorious Record of 120,000 American Men, Women and Children.

LIBERTY ENLIGHTENING THE WORLD.

LIBERTY'S BIRTH.

And the Genius to Whom the Great Work Owes Its Origin.

BEGINNING THE WORK.

The day of the dedication ceremony finally arrived.

The day itself, October 28, 1886, was rainy, blustery, and cold. In spite of the weather, thousands lined the four-mile parade route, which started at Fifth Avenue and 57th Street, detoured around broken pavement over to Madison Avenue, and then went down Broadway to the Battery at the tip of Manhattan. French and American flags hung from every building along the way. Honored guests on the reviewing stand remained standing during the whole parade because the upholstered seats provided for them were soaked from the rain.

The last units passed by at about one o'clock, at the same time the nautical parade started. At a gun signal, more than three hundred ships fell in line and started moving slowly through fog down the Hudson River from the area of the 42nd Street pier. They were to form a crescent in the harbor below Bedloe's Island.

Carriages transported President Grover Cleveland and special dignitaries to the dock where they boarded the *Dispatch*. As their boat passed in front of the American and French warships, the president was given a twenty-one gun salute. Smoke mixed with fog allowed those on shore only a hazy picture of what was happening.

The *Dispatch* was too large to come alongside the pier at Bedloe's Island. The president had to transfer to a launch that, in turn, discharged him onto a float, and from there a ladder

The inauguration of the statue.

led to the pier. President Cleveland, being of ample proportions, required considerable assistance to gain the next level. It seemed probable that his dignity might be lost in a wet landing.

The speaker's platform was festooned with red, white, and blue bunting. Top hats were the order of the day, but not a single female had been invited for the final event. The excuse given for this was that the crush of people in such a small area would make it unsafe for the delicate sex. Responding to their exclusion, a group of fashionably dressed women hired their own launch. It was small enough to weave in and around the official vessels. This assured them a share of attention and a better view of the events than many of their husbands, who had wangled invitations to be on the island for the big moment.

A band was playing as the crowd gathered. A minister gave the invocation. Ferdinand de Lesseps spoke for the Union Franco-Americaine. There were shouts from people insisting they hear from Bartholdi himself. He had not been scheduled to speak, as he was on his way to the crown of the statue where he was to perform the climax of the celebration—the removal of a huge flag of France that covered Liberty's face. A young boy had been stationed at the side of the platform. He was to give the signal when the speeches were over.

Senator William Evarts had the honor of giving the last speech on the program. He paused after the third paragraph of his speech. The young boy thought this pause was the conclusion and he gave the signal. Bartholdi pulled the flag in through the openings of Liberty's crown. There was shouting. Pandemonium broke out as the ships in the harbor blasted their salute.

Senator Evarts was not to be stopped, however. He turned his back on the cheering audience and continued to give his speech directly to the president. President Cleveland was at a loss whether to listen to Evarts or join the milling throng now surging toward the base of the pedestal. But no one was allowed inside.

Now the rush centered on trying to get back to the boats. Everyone was afraid he'd be left stranded on the island. The crush was terrible. "Outrageous," the newspapers reported. A group of New York City aldermen got on the wrong boat, and the people who embarked on the aldermen's boat ate all the food that had been prepared for the celebration. All in all, it was a day to remember—and, for some, to forget!

The great night of fireworks and the lighting of the statue was postponed because of the weather, and rescheduled for November 1. Bartholdi and his wife missed the celebration because they had accepted an invitation to board a special railroad car as guests of the Union League Club and the New York Central Railroad to view Niagara Falls.

When they returned, Bartholdi went to inspect the statue at night. He was very disappointed. There was a circle of colored lights at the base that lit the pedestal rather than the statue itself. From the shore, someone said, the statue looked more like a glowworm than a lighthouse. It would take another generation to do the Lady justice.

◄ *The celebration of Lady Liberty was the news of the day.*

HER
FIRST
HUNDRED
YEARS

Liberty Enlightening the World—the official name for the statue—was not news anymore. Joseph Pulitzer had to find other headlines to boost the circulation of *The World*. Outside of New York, the country was only mildly interested in the statue. Bartholdi had been right when he wrote that the American character "is hardly open to things of the imagination."

But as Liberty's penny-bright sparkle tarnished to a soft mellow green, there were others who were to place a higher value upon her. These were the immigrants who were arriving in waves from every corner of Europe. Nearly five million came in the 1880s. Their first stop in America was at Castle Garden, at the tip of Manhattan, to have their papers and health checked.

In 1892 an impressive brick building was built just across a narrow channel of water from the Lady. It became known as Ellis Island, named after the original owner of the property. In those days there was no way to approach this island other than by water. New York harbor was by far the busiest port of entry.

The Statue of Liberty was the first landmark these new arrivals saw from the railings of their ships. She held her arm up as if to say, "This way, please." She was truly the "Mother of Exiles." Forty percent of all Americans today can trace their ancestry through Ellis Island.

Free people are seldom the best judge of freedom. These newcomers pointed out the true meaning of liberty to Americans who had taken it for granted. Freedom for these individuals meant not to be hungry or afraid. These emotions were not the same as those envisioned by Bartholdi, or Pulitzer, or any of the privileged few who had dropped their calling cards in the cornerstone at Liberty's feet.

The immigrants came with patience and forbearance. They saw the promise of a wonderful future rather than a confirmation that life would immediately offer everything to them. If they were not able to make their fortune at once, there was a chance their children would in the years to come.

New arrivals on an ocean steamer passing the Lady in 1887.

Emma Lazarus was a young New York–born poet who had expressed in a poem what the statue meant even before Liberty had reached America.

The New Colossus

Not like the brazen giant of Greek fame,
With conquering limbs astride from land to land;
Here at the sea-washed, sunset gates shall stand
A mighty woman with a torch, whose flame
Is the imprisoned lightning, and her name
Mother of Exiles. From her beacon-hand
Glows world-wide welcome; her mild eyes command
The air-bridged harbor that twin cities frame.
"Keep, ancient lands, your storied pomp!" cries she
With silent lips. "Give me your tired, your poor,
Your huddled masses yearning to breathe free,
The wretched refuse of your teeming shore.
Send these, the homeless, tempest-tost, to me,
I lift my lamp beside the golden door!"

Emma Lazarus.

In all the flourish and fanfare of building the pedestal, these words had been filed away in an obscure volume of verse written to aid fund-raising back in 1883. The poem had been read by a few people and even praised by James Russell Lowell, the esteemed poet.

Emma Lazarus was the daughter of a wealthy Jewish family that could trace its prominence in New York back to colonial times. Although Emma had lived a sheltered life, she had been touched by the shocking news of the persecution of Jews in tsarist Russia. Nothing in her experience could have given her a taste of the suffering these people had endured in their fight for freedom and liberty, but in her poem she breathed life into the words "yearning to breathe free."

In 1901 there had been a change in the order of management of the statue. The lighthouse commission had strongly advised that the torch be extinguished. It was no longer useful to ship navigation, they said. The light went out completely in March

Ellis Island in its heyday.

1902. Surprisingly, complaints came from enraged citizens all over the country. Finally President Theodore Roosevelt ordered that the property be transferred to the War Department, which would come up with a budget to keep the light burning for sentiment's sake.

Some time during the transfer of the property, sixteen years after Emma Lazarus's death, a bronze plaque was placed on an interior wall of the pedestal, engraved with the words of her poem. No one knows who was responsible for the memorial. It occurred in 1903, when immigration was at its peak. Emma's words pointed out the meaning of liberty to Americans who had forgotten their own flight for freedom. A dozen or more years had made the difference between headlines and history. America had finally adopted the gift from France.

The statue gained a significance of which its creator had never dreamed. This should have softened Bartholdi's bitterness, caused by his belief that he had not been fairly paid for his grandiose work of art. So much of his time had been involved in the creation of the statue that his other work had been neglected.

In a letter to Joseph Pulitzer dated a year after the statue's dedication, Bartholdi unloaded his complaints to his friend. "Last year much was spoken about American gratitude towards me. It was said Congress would vote me an award in consideration of all the great sacrifices which I have had to bear."

Pulitzer turned a deaf ear. He had had enough problems trying to raise money for the acceptance of the statue. He didn't see how Bartholdi could expect more from the people of the United States. Pulitzer had already spent a thousand dollars of the pedestal fund to present the sculptor with a handsome trophy designed in the Tiffany studios.

The trophy was a large silver globe with the torch of Liberty at the North Pole. France and the main rivers of the world were inlaid in gold. Bartholdi's head in relief faced America from the Pacific Ocean. The base was of petrified wood with two inscriptions: "All Homage and Thanks to the Great Sculptor Bartholdi" and "A Tribute from the *New York World* and Over 121,000 Americans to Auguste Bartholdi and the Great Liberty-Loving People of France."

It was an impressive gift, but not what Bartholdi had hoped for. His work on the great statue had not even brought him other commissions. The Lafayette Monument he had proposed for the front of the White House had been denied him. In France he had been decorated as a commander in the Legion of Honor, but he would have preferred a cash settlement there too.

Bartholdi returned to America only once more in 1893. He had come to see about his patent rights. Every souvenir shop in New York City had a stock of miniature statues. He had written a friend that he hoped there would be a demand for his own models produced in France, "which may help to make up for the large sacrifices that, as you personally so well know, had to be made by me." An injunction was brought against one manufacturer, restraining him from selling the bronze imitations, but it hardly slowed the traffic in these souvenirs.

Bartholdi was to complete one other significant monument—a double statue of the Marquis de Lafayette and George Washington which today stands in the Place des Etats-Unis in Paris. An exact replica was placed in New York City at the corner of Manhattan Avenue and 114th Street.

The last piece Bartholdi worked on was his own memorial monument, which represented a figure holding out a laurel wreath. He had been sick and knew he was about to die. The end came on the morning of October 4, 1904. Bartholdi was seventy years old.

Bartholdi would have been proud of the eulogy that praised his talents, but he would have

Lafayette Monument.

been prouder still to know that his statue had taken on a life of her own. As one writer said, "The more the Statue belonged to mankind, the more American it grew."

Liberty sent many messages out to the world. She guarded a forceful, free country, a country made strong through years of peace. Europe had never been so lucky.

In 1916, Woodrow Wilson declared, "There has come more and more into my heart the conviction that peace is going to come to the world only with liberty." Those words were spoken at the dedication of a new system of floodlights for the Statue of Liberty. The statue had been designed before the advent of electric lights. Kerosene lanterns were to have radiated from her crown. Bartholdi had made the suggestion that the windows of the crown should be covered with colored glass and illuminated from within. At the last minute an electric generating system had been added to the original plans of the statue.

Her nighttime display had always been a disappointment, but now that technology had made so much progress, it was time to see what could be done for the Lady.

Her torch had never even remotely looked like a flame. Even with gilding, the light reflected from lighting below barely showed the outline. Gutzon Borglum, sculptor of Mount Rushmore, was commissioned to cut out most of the copper torch and install cathedral glass in large squares. For the first time, the torch would be lit from the inside. A new $30,000 system of floodlights, made by General Electric, was installed at her base. She also had her first cosmetic cleaning. Carefully, so as not to disturb the protective patina, she was given her first and only steam bath.

The ceremony to show off her new look was a fine, elaborate affair. Chauncey Depew was the only speaker who had also been present at the unveiling in 1886, but there were younger orators who sang Liberty's praises. And this time women were invited to take part in the program.

While speakers on the flag-draped stand below strained to watch, a light plane named *Liberty,* piloted by a woman, circled the statue. After many years of neglect, the statue was now remembered, refurbished, and rededicated.

One of Liberty's greatest jobs was still ahead of her. Two months after her torch was lit, Germany announced that she would conduct unrestricted submarine warfare on all ships carrying supplies to England and the Allies. This put American ships and lives in jeopardy. America was involved whether she liked it or not. The United States declared war on Germany on April 6, 1917.

"For the right is more precious than peace," the president said.

The symbol of liberty was now the symbol of unity. She was the patriotic call to arms. There were Liberty postal cards, watch fobs, plates, and satin pillows. Her picture was on the bonds that were helping finance the war and buy guns for our soldiers.

Remember Your First Thrill of AMERICAN LIBERTY

YOUR DUTY-Buy
United States Government Bonds
2ⁿᵈ Liberty Loan of 1917

The statue was used to call Americans to their patriotic duty.

Troops on ships saluted the statue as they sailed abroad. Later, soldiers who had gone through a living hell broke into tears when they sighted her on their return. Seeing her meant they were home, whether home was a prairie state or the mountains of the West or the teeming city at Liberty's feet. She *was* America. She was the Lady for whom they were fighting.

The soldiers returned home to prosperity—for the time being. It was a prosperity to be guarded jealously. United States citizens—formerly immigrants—who had known Ellis Island well a generation ago now lobbied for laws to restrict others from seeking these same opportunities. If Americans were to have the freedom to earn a good living, they felt, the freedom of immigrants to enter the United States and take over their jobs had to be denied.

The year 1924, when the statue was declared a national monument, was also the year a quota system was established. This limited the number of immigrants allowed to enter the United States from various countries to the percentage of the ethnic makeup of the country at the time. A literacy test—given in English—was required of each immigrant.

The flow of new arrivals slowed to a trickle, and when the United States suffered the economic crash of 1929, the arrival of immigrants dried up almost entirely. People felt they could starve just as well where they were.

Even during the depths of the Great Depression, people worried about the Lady. It was reported there were bad shadows under her chin and around her eyes, caused by the torch. Under her nose an ugly blur was cast on either side of her face, giving her cheeks a hollow appearance.

People couldn't let the old girl age without grace. A new floodlighting system was installed by Westinghouse Electric to be inaugurated on October 28, her forty-fifth birthday. The celebration was moved ahead two days though, so that visiting Mlle. José Laval, the daughter of France's premier, could turn on the lights.

Mlle. Laval stood on the observatory level of the Empire State Building, which now dwarfed the Lady in height. The French woman waved her hand over an electric eye and, in a show of modern technology, Miss Liberty glowed with light, not one shadow encircling her staring eyes.

In 1933 the statue again changed guardians. She was placed under the jurisdiction of the National Park Service, which still maintains her grounds and image. It was the Park Service's job to start planning for Liberty's fiftieth jubilee.

In 1936 peace was only a word. The world of Sheila Jane Crooke, a poet from Illinois, was not the same one Emma Lazarus had known. The poet, who earned first prize in the contest to honor Liberty, phrased it well.

In London I talked to a woman who'd just received a government gas mask. "Do you think," I said, "that you'll ever use that?"

She shook her head.

"I don't know," she answered. "I don't know, but I'm afraid." I'm afraid, they said. I'm afraid, I'm afraid.

When we steamed into New York harbor the other day I got up very early.

So as to be sure of getting a good, long look at Liberty, standing there.

So proud, so peacefully reassuring, so . . .

God bless you, old girl! So unafraid!

On the day of rededication, President Franklin Delano Roosevelt came to Bedloe's Island to deliver a speech. Not as many people were on hand as had been at the statue's unveiling, but Roosevelt's words were broadcast by radio to millions of listeners.

"Grover Cleveland, president of the United States, accepted this gift with the pledge that 'we will not forget that liberty has here made her home; nor shall her chosen altar be neglected,' " Roosevelt declared. "During those fifty years that covenant between ourselves and our most cherished convictions has not been broken."

He spoke too about the unity of Americans bound together by the hope of a common future rather than by reverence for a common past.

In 1941 that future was threatened. War was declared when the United States was attacked by the Japanese at Pearl Harbor. The unified effort of every citizen in the country was required to mobilize for war.

Miss Liberty was in the news again as the symbol that whipped people's emotions into a display of patriotic generosity. The symbol came to life in the form of a young woman dressed in a Roman toga, with a spiked crown on her head and carrying a torch. She traveled across the country selling war bonds. She and Uncle Sam marched down just about every main street in the United States.

In New York City the *World Telegram* ran this headline: "The Lady Has a Daughter." She was white plaster and one-third the size of her "mother," but she stood proudly in Times Square with her torch lit as a promotional stunt, again to sell war bonds.

Out in the harbor the real Liberty was darkened in the blackout. Europe had seemed far away in 1886, but now long-range bombers could cross the Atlantic in hours. Liberty was there to welcome friends, not to light the way for an enemy. The blackout was lifted only twice during the war. At midnight on New Year's Eve in 1943, Liberty's torch flashed

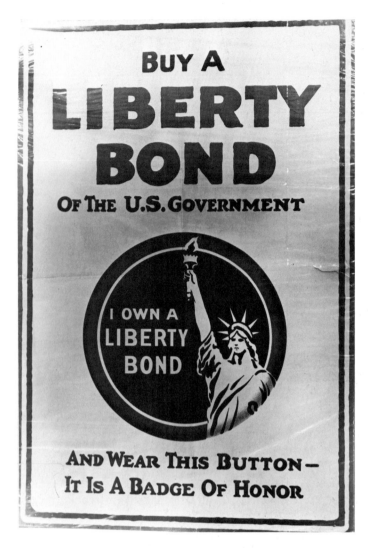

BUY A LIBERTY BOND OF THE U.S. GOVERNMENT

I OWN A LIBERTY BOND

AND WEAR THIS BUTTON— IT IS A BADGE OF HONOR

three dots and a dash, the Morse code for V as in victory. On D-day, June 6, 1945, the torch flashed again. This time people knew peace would come soon. The world could not stand much more punishment.

Veterans returned. Families tried to put the pieces of their lives back together again. Travel was possible once more. Those coming to visit the statue were ashamed at the neglect they saw. Trash littered the grounds. Thoughtless tourists had scribbled their names on the stone pedestal. A new effort was sponsored to give Liberty a special grooming.

The army tore down the obsolete buildings no longer in use on the island. Bartholdi's monument had occupied only a part of the island's twelve acres. The American Scenic and Historic Preservation Society suggested that a new museum be housed in the base of the statue. It would commemorate the contributions of immigrants to the American way of life.

In 1955, one year after Ellis Island was officially closed as an immigration center, funds were collected to create such a museum on Bedloe's Island. This time the public's generosity was spurred by sentiment.

In 1956 the name Bedloe's Island was changed to Liberty Island. Bartholdi's statue had left her imprint on America's geography as well as on her population.

Over the years a few lucky people have had this famous island as their home address. The first child to be born there was named Liberty. A more recent resident is Jim Hill. He was born in 1925 in a house near the statue's base. Hill's father ran the island's concession stand. Jim Hill is now the manager of that stand.

There weren't many other children to play with on the island when Hill was growing up, but his mainland friends thought it wonderful to go to school by boat and to be able to

From any angle and at all times,
the Statue of Liberty is an awesome sight.

Illuminated at night, the Lady is inspiring.

THE GREAT BARTHOLDI STATUE,
LIBERTY ENLIGHTENING THE WORLD.
THE GIFT OF FRANCE TO THE AMERICAN PEOPLE.
ERECTED ON BEDLOE'S ISLAND NEW YORK HARBOR UNVEILED OCT. 28TH 1886

This magnificent colossal Statue (the largest ever known in the World) is of copper bronzed 151 feet in height and is mounted on a Stone Pedestal 154 feet high, making the extreme height from foundation of Pedestal to the torch 305 feet. the height of the Statue from the heel to the top of the head is 111 ft. 6 in. Length of the hand 16 feet. Head from chin to cranium 17ft 3in. Breadth from ear to ear 10 feet, Length of nose 4ft 6in Length of right arm 42 feet. Circumference of arm 12 feet, Width of mouth 3 feet, Weight of Statue 450,000 pounds (225 tons) 40 persons can stand comfortably in the head and the torch will hold 12 people The torch at night displays a powerful electric light and the great Statue thus presents by night as by day an exceedingly grand and imposing appearance.

This Currier & Ives of the statue was commissioned one hundred years ago to raise funds for the statue's pedestal and assembly.

Ellis Island was the first stop for immigrants to this country.

Scaffolding has completely encased the statue in preparation for work to be done before the Lady's 100th anniversary in 1986.

Work on the new torch is being carried out in workshops at the base of the statue.

New Jersey views the backside of Liberty—and isn't too happy about it!

There is even a store in New York City that sells only statue memorabilia.

Liberty has played a starring role in many films, including Funny Girl *and* Yankee Doodle Dandy.

play around the huge toy in the backyard. "It's always been a part of my life," Hill admits with pride.

David Moffitt is the superintendent of Liberty and Ellis islands for the National Park Service. He sees the statue in all kinds of weather. Occasionally a bad nor'easter will seal off the island, but when the ferries are running, there are sure to be tourists aboard.

"Sometimes, in early evenings, right after one of those flash rains," Moffitt says, "Liberty turns eight to ten shades of green, from emerald to very dark. When the sun comes out, she just glistens."

In 1965 Ellis Island was made part of the Liberty National Monument. Rejuvenation of this site was to be deferred, but not forgotten. That same year, President Lyndon Johnson called for the passage of a new, fairer immigration bill that would do away with the national-origins quota system. Acceptance would be based on the skills of the applicant.

The Statue of Liberty received its biggest scare in 1965. A group of conspirators threatened to blow her up if the country didn't change its foreign policy. They were protesting that U.S. troops were in Vietnam and that U.S. ties had been cut with Cuba. It shocked most of the country that anyone would dare destroy the symbol of all the good things America had done in the world.

The guilty parties were punished. Liberty remained unscathed, except for the damage age had caused. This damage was becoming more and more apparent as thoughts turned to the grand affair of the statue's one hundredth birthday.

RESTORATION

I t seems fitting that it was a Frenchman who discovered how much help Ms. Liberty needed to restore her health in time for her centennial on October 28, 1986. Everyone had thought she was doing quite well for her age. She had withstood hurricane-force winds sweeping in from the Atlantic, which buffeted her with saltwater spray. She had survived an even more serious and particularly modern affliction, constant exposure to air pollution.

Her green patina, which was acquired in the first year, actually had protected her complexion. The green oxidation is a kind of rust. Once the first layer of copper has gone through the change, it seals itself off from further damage.

Minor repairs to the statue had taken place over the years, but they had been done on a piecemeal basis without any long-range plan.

It was Jacques Moutard, a metallurgical engineer, who diagnosed Liberty's condition. He had been assigned the job of restoring a small statue on Mont Auxois in France. The sculptor of that monument, Jean Francoise Millet, had used the same techniques and materials that had been used to construct Liberty. Moutard found the Millet statue in very poor condition. It was rusting away from the inside at such an alarming rate that it was in danger of toppling from its foundation. Moutard couldn't help wonder what was happening to the much larger copper-and-iron monument in New York harbor.

In 1980, Moutard discussed his concern with the French philanthropist Philippe Vallery-Radot, who was providing funds for the restoration of the Millet statue. The men thought it was a wonderful idea to offer assistance in renovating France's gift in time for Liberty's one hundredth birthday.

Vallery-Radot wrote to officials of the National Park Service, Liberty's guardian. Arrangements were made for Moutard to inspect the statue. Philippe Grandjean, a Paris architect who had considerable experience in metal research and restoring antique structures, accompanied him.

UNCLE SAM CONGRATULATES MISS LIBERTY.

As this newspaper cartoon shows, in 1885—just as in 1985—many groups of people contributed to restoring Liberty's health.

The men discovered what they suspected to be true: outwardly the statue seemed to have carried her age well, but her interior needed attention. Two more Frenchmen, a structural engineer and a specialist in mechanical and electrical matters, joined them.

As soon as their early analysis of the problems was delivered to the American government, things began to happen. Everyone concerned was shocked that the statue had been left untouched for so long. Plans for a complete renovation were drawn up. Liberty was too valuable a possession to let rust away until her health was beyond repair.

The restoration team was joined by a group of American experts. A well-established architectural firm, Swanke Hayden Connell, was chosen to draw up plans to conform to American standards and deal with contractors. The firm had been in charge of the restoration of the original United States Senate and Supreme Court chambers. Its staff would work directly with the French group, sharing equal authority. Thierry Despont, a French architect with offices in New York, joined the team to act as interpreter.

Here was a group of experts, each with different experience, all working toward the same goal. Although there were frequently different opinions about the methods to be used to attain that goal, more cooperation seemed to exist in the twentieth century than back in the days when Bartholdi was trying to put together a working team.

Despont points out, "On the one extreme, you have someone like Moutard, who is really the old style, Old World craftsman. He is quiet and he knows his craft. He can look at the statue and feel what's wrong with it. He can't necessarily explain it, but he knows how to repair it.

"And then on the other extreme, you have Swanke Hayden Connell, which is one of the largest architectural firms in the country and is geared to the production of large office buildings. . . . They're known for their competence and efficiency at producing things on time. The individuals on the project have all shared a kind of romantic enthusiasm for the job that has gotten us over all discrepancies in communicating and arguing so far."

In addition to the working team of experts, an advisory committee was set up for consultation. Fifteen contractors are involved.

In May, 1982, President Ronald Reagan announced the formation of the Statue of Liberty–Ellis Island Centennial Commission with businessman Lee A. Iacocca as its chairman. Other well-known American personalities, Bob Hope among them, were enlisted to help raise funds for the project.

As with the original statue and pedestal, all funds are coming from private sources. No taxpayers' money is being used to supply the $29 million it is estimated will be spent to ready the statue for her 1986 celebration.

Large corporations are giving gifts. Schoolchildren are coming up with ideas to raise money. Contributors' names are being listed on a commemorative scroll. All these people are guaranteeing that Ms. Liberty will be healthier and stronger than ever on her hundredth birthday.

The biggest disappointment to the renovation team was that no original drawings of the statue existed. Searching for the records, they discovered that a fire at the studio of Gaget, Gauthier and Company, where the statue was constructed, had destroyed all the working sheets. Only a few drawings from Eiffel's architectural firm were found.

One mystery was never solved. Eiffel's original design had been altered during construction, but no one knows why. The change shifted the supports of the upraised arm, which holds the torch, eighteen inches to the side and slightly forward. This put an added strain on the shoulder truss. The weakened connection has caused problems. It had been repaired several times, but for many years the ladder to the torch has been closed to the public. Only a maintenance crew is allowed to go to the top.

The question of who ordered the change was raised. Most theorists are sure the greatest French engineer of the nineteenth century would not have made such a clumsy miscalculation. He was a perfectionist. Most likely the modification was made at the time the copper sheathing was installed. Perhaps one of the thin molds had been flattened during transport so that an on-the-job change was required. Perhaps the order was given by Bartholdi himself to give the statue a better angle of design.

Ross Holland, the foundation's director of restoration and preservation, felt that the first order of business was to keep Liberty's right arm from tilting. However, the team decided to leave her the way she is. A few new supports relieved the stress on the arm. The shoulder was repaired, not rebuilt.

Eiffel's drawings also show that the position of the head was shifted about two feet during construction. Because of this misalignment, one of the seven spikes in the statue's crown has rubbed against her shoulder. To remedy this problem, a very slight nudge moved the spike a few millimeters. The crew depressed the skin in a shallow dimple to make sure there would be no more rubbing. Liberty's head will remain at the same familiar angle.

After months of consultation, the scaffolding began to rise. The entire statue was caged in a delicate yet sturdy mesh of metal framework. Some very sophisticated techniques that would have seemed miraculous at the time of Liberty's construction are being used to keep her looking her same sedate self. Through modern know-how, experts on both sides of the Atlantic are keeping up-to-date on the progress of the work. They can be consulted without leaving their respective offices.

The work is being monitored on two continents by a video communications network linking Liberty Island, Manhattan, and Paris. Portable video cameras can be focused on any part of the statue, inside or out. A call can be sent to all offices.

Scaffolding of the pedestal. ▶

A video camera scans a problem area, for instance, and almost immediately the picture flashes on screens before the experts. If they want a printout of a still image, they have only to program their monitor to make one. The advice given is just as well considered as if consultation had taken place on the spot.

Whenever any work is being done on the skin of the statue, craftsmen are positioned at the same point inside, hanging from pulley-adjusted sling seats, and outside, on the scaffold. They are in constant communication via walkie-talkies.

The statue was wired for everything but sound, but her creaks and groans were already being monitored by the scaffold crew. To measure wind speed, anemometers were placed on the torch and at the foot of the statue. The Lady has withstood some severe weather in her time, but this was the first time that those forces had been accurately analyzed. It was found that her torch-holding arm sometimes swung in a fifteen-inch arc.

Engineers installed devices to measure temperature and humidity inside the shell to see how they could avoid further rusting of the sturdy skeleton. They discovered the temperature inside the statue at times could reach 120° Fahrenheit in the summer. Carbon dioxide levels, caused by her hundreds of visitors, are sometimes dangerously high. Another set of instruments measures the flow of air. Were there dead areas and draft areas?

To calculate how the statue reacted to all these changes, one hundred forty-two stress gauges were installed on different parts of her internal structure to record how she moved under heavy wind conditions and sudden changes in temperature. It was as if a team of doctors was taking her pulse every minute.

All of Liberty's measurements were fed into a computer-aided design program devised by the American Society of Civil Engineers. The result will be a modern system of interior climate control.

Not only is Liberty being saved by modern science, she is also helping scientists in their research to learn new ways to work out difficult problems in building renovation. One example is how to get rid of seven layers of paint that had been applied at one time or another to the inside of the shell.

At first this didn't seem like such a difficult problem, but it turned out to be bothersome. One of the layers was a black coal-tar paint that had been used as a sealant between the copper sections to keep the statue waterproof. Anything that would dissolve the mixture and let it run between the cracks would have seriously damaged Liberty's complexion. Chemical stripping also posed health hazards for workers in such a confined space. Sand blasting would weaken some of the sharper folds in the statue.

Ten different methods were tested for removing the gummy coating and succeeding layers of paint. Spraying with ice, sand, glass balls, hot air, even using crushed walnut shells, were all tried.

The team finally chose to give the statue a deep-freeze treatment with liquid nitrogen at 350° below zero. This technique freezes and shrinks the paint rather than dissolving it. The heavy layers peeled right off. The final coal-tar undercoating was removed by gentle blasting using baking soda instead of sand.

"There will be benefits throughout the industry from this project," said Lawrence Bellante, one of the engineers. "This novel way of freezing the paint is an inexpensive process that contractors will undoubtedly be using to restore delicate parts of old buildings in the future. Window frames often have to be replaced. Liberty has shown them a way to save time, money, and materials."

The nitrogen did not work on the iron skeleton, however. Instead, the painting contractor adapted an existing system which enables the paint to be blasted off and the particles immediately vacuumed up by a hose surrounding the blasting tube, sort of like a dentist's drill.

Although the surface of Liberty's skin was in fairly good condition, there were small areas that had to be patched. Over the years, water had collected in the folds of Liberty's robe and the curls of her hair. Bell Laboratories needed to know more about the long-term effects of corrosion on copper, which is used in communications and electronics equipment. They offered the use of their sophisticated laboratory equipment. They wanted the chance to study parts of the statue's skin that have corroded naturally at different rates under various weather conditions.

In return for using Liberty as a research project, Bell Labs is donating a large green copper roof from its Murray Hill, New Jersey, laboratories for the patching. New copper would be as bright as a penny. It would take too long for the natural patina to form. Artificially creating the patina with acid solutions would probably form structural weak points. This treatment is supposed to last for years. The renovation team felt fortunate that copper of just the right grade, thickness, and age could be found. They've tried to make all substitutions in materials as close to the original ones as possible.

The iron used in the bars and saddles supporting the copper was analyzed thoroughly. It was made by an old formula. It is called puddled iron, and is similar to wrought iron. It gives a certain flexibility to the structure. The experts started looking for a new material that would not make the statue any more rigid or supple, but would be rustproof and at the same time compatible with the copper. There is an electrolytic reaction between the copper and iron when they touch that has rusted the iron.

Liberty's real problem was found in the connecting bars. They are a web of horizontal and vertical iron belts that follow exactly the interior of the statue, but theoretically do not quite touch it. The belts are connected to the skin through riveted copper saddles with an insulating material that helps keep the metals apart. No two armatures (protective covering) are alike. As the insulation has worn away, the rust has taken over. This has caused at least a third of the rivets to break away from the skin.

The experts wanted to use an iron armature if possible to copy Eiffel's plan, but they wanted to replace the insulation with something better. Chemists came up with a solution.

The most time-consuming job was the replacement of almost sixteen hundred pieces of this iron web, with no two pieces being alike. What could modern science come up with to make the job easier? All sorts of schemes were proposed. The most complicated technique, using space-age technology, was to take photographs of each separate piece from at least three sides at once. These photos were to be fed into a computer that would memorize every curve and dimension, and then build three-dimensional models using a robot arm to cut the pictures into wax. These would be used as molds to cast the final replacement parts.

Other experts suggested laser scanning and fiberglass wet casts. They finally found a simple nineteenth-century technique that was more efficient.

A skilled craftsman was hoisted on a sling inside the statue. With a soft piece of metal, he hammered away, using his eye and his judgment to make a duplicate. When this was finished, it served as a template for a piece made from heavier metal. Eiffel and Bartholdi would have understood and approved this process.

These pieces had to be duplicated before they were removed. Great care was taken to remove only four at a time. An elaborate schedule was programmed by computer, so that the four pieces were always taken from four different levels and from four different sides of the statue. This was further proof that Eiffel's original design had been worked out as a finely integrated unit where stresses balanced throughout the structure.

Although almost all of the armature bars and saddles are being replaced, there was a request that, for historical value, a few of the original ones be saved. This has been done. In the heel of the statue's right foot, the original ironwork of the 1880s has been preserved.

The only part of the statue that had to be completely replaced was the torch. The most exposed part of the statue, it is hit by the worst weather, from below as well as from all sides. Since holes were cut in the flame to insert yellow cathedral glass, the torch has continually leaked, causing extensive rusting. In making the new torch, there was no sense in copying old mistakes.

This time the flame will be a solid copper piece, gilded and illuminated from the outside by powerful spotlights.

The only part of the statue that had to be completely replaced was the torch.

As seems fitting, the work on the torch is being carried out by a team of ten French artisans who are copying every detail of the original. Graceful acanthus leaves and miniature ears of corn, the exact duplicate of the first design, are being etched on the balcony of the torch.

The new flame is being hammered by hand, just as it was a century ago. Les Metalliers Champenois of Reims, France, is making a plaster of paris mold from the existing flame. A wooden mold of thin strips of lath was fitted together. The copper was placed inside the mold and hammered carefully to follow the exact contour of the original.

Visitors have been able to watch the job in progress in workshops near the base of the statue. The torch will be bolted to the statue's right hand just before the birthday celebration. The easiest way to do this job is by helicopter. Frédéric Auguste Bartholdi would have been amazed.

Everything is being done to ease the crowds of tourists who are bound to come to see Liberty's new look. If the restoration effort has been a success, the old girl will look much the same. There will be real changes only on the inside of the pedestal.

Several concrete floors in the stone base have been eliminated. They had nothing to do with the support of the structure and only crammed the passageway. Now a dramatic space has been opened up, a towering cave that seems to stretch upward forever.

A brand-new elevator, the largest in the world, is being designed to take tourists from ground level to the foot of the statue. This double-decked hydraulic lift will rise on a shaft with no cables. It will be glass on all sides. Special lights on the elevator itself will illuminate whatever it is passing to give a dramatic effect.

"The shadows will be dynamic," said Robert Landsman, of the architectural firm Swanke Hayden Connell.

Passengers will step out at the colonnade level near the top of the pedestal. One flight above, a new mezzanine level has been constructed, where visitors will step into the top of the elevator for the descent and exit. More people will be moved in and out of the monument with greater ease and comfort than ever before.

The actual climb starts at the mezzanine floor. One hundred sixty-eight steps wind upward to the head of the statue.

There will be new stainless steel stairs for the statue's pedestal and new treads and railing for the two spiral staircases that reach the crown. The stairs are divided for one-way traffic with rest stops for the weary. Nothing has been done to ease this part of the tour.

"Thirty years afterward, people remember the grueling climb to the top," says Richard Hayden of Swanke Hayden Connell. "The National Park Service wanted to preserve it. We agreed."

The old screening around the pylon has been removed and the lighting improved. Climbers will have a much better view of Liberty than ever before. They will be able to appreciate how well the designs of Bartholdi, Eiffel, and Hunt mesh together.

An emergency elevator will run from the bottom of the pedestal to just below the head. It will ride on geared tracks like a window-washer's lift.

With so many tourists from around the world coming her way in 1986, Liberty is expected to turn into a super money-maker. That's one reason why there's an argument now over her address. It may be the biggest custody battle ever.

The citizens of New Jersey want to claim the statue as theirs. They have some compelling arguments. Technically, Liberty Island and Ellis Island do lie on the New Jersey side of the state line, which runs down the middle of the Hudson River. But in 1834 an agreement was reached to give both islands a New York address. No one particularly cared back then. However, the state that has the final legal claim collects millions of dollars in annual sales tax receipts and income tax revenues generated by the thousands who visit the sites. With a boom in tourism expected when the statue reopens in the summer of 1986, it is a sum well worth fighting for.

"New York City makes money, and all we get is a lot of carbon monoxide," complains Jean Scanlon, an aide to Jersey City's former mayor, Gerald McCann.

New Jersey also argues that they provide power, water, and phone services to the sites, and eighty-eight percent of Ellis Island is built on landfill made from New Jersey dirt. New York Governor Mario Cuomo plans to fight the case being brought to court.

In jest, the lawyers for New Jersey say that if they lose the case, they'll revive a 1968 move in the state legislature to turn the statue around so that New Jersey can see her face, not her back.

From whatever view the Statue of Liberty is seen, she is an impressive monument. America claims her, but as the author O'Henry pointed out, she has a cosmopolitan makeup.

> Made by an Italian [as Bartholdi's name implies, his ancestors came from Italy] and presented to the American people on behalf of the French government for the purpose of welcoming Irish immigrants into the Dutch city of New York.

On her fiftieth birthday, the magic of radio enabled the North American continent to listen to the celebration. On her hundredth birthday, the whole world can join in. Televised pictures will be beamed via a satellite receiving and sending station in outer space. Who knows what the next hundred years will bring? But it's almost a sure thing that Miss Liberty will still be standing in New York harbor as a symbol of a great idea that may one day spread throughout the world.

SOME INTERESTING MEASUREMENTS OF THE STATUE OF LIBERTY:

★ If the statue and her pedestal were laid flat on the ground, they wouldn't quite fit on a football field (305′6″).

★ She weighs as much as a herd of forty-five full-grown elephants (225 tons).

★ Her right arm stretches more than four stories above her shoulder (42′).

★ The tablet she holds is bigger than the average room in a house (13′7″ × 23′7″).

★ Her mouth is as wide as a yardstick is long.

★ Her fingernail is bigger than the biggest picture book on your shelf (13″ × 10″).

★ Liberty's hand is as long as the height of three people laid end to end (16′5″) and one finger might reach from the floor to the ceiling of your room (8′).

BIBLIOGRAPHY

Allen, Frederick. "Saving the Statue." *American Heritage* 35, no. 4 (June/July 1984): 97–109.

Bell, James B. and Richard I. Abrams. *In Search of Liberty.* Garden City, New York: Doubleday & Company, Inc., 1984.

Ferretti, Fred. "A Splendid Restoration Begins." *Travel & Leisure* 14, no. 7 (July 1984).

Gschaedler, Andre. *True Light on the Statue of Liberty and Its Creator:* Narbeth, Pennsylvania: Livingston Publishing Co., 1966.

Handlin, Oscar and the editors of Newsweek Book Division. *Statue of Liberty.* New York: Newsweek, 1971.

Heidish, Marcy. "The Grande Dame of the Harbor." *Geo* 6, no. 7 (July 1984): 36–45.

Kraske, Robert. *The Statue of Liberty Comes to America.* Easton, Maryland: Garrard, 1972.

Mercer, Charles. *Statue of Liberty.* New York: G. P. Putnam's Sons, 1985.

Miller, Natalie. *Story of the Statue of Liberty.* Chicago: Children's Press, 1965.

Nason, Thelma. *Our Statue of Liberty.* Cleveland: Modern Curriculum, 1969.

Our Gift from France: The Story of the Great Liberty Statue. Woodbury, New Jersey: Gloucester County Historical Society, 1976.

Pauli, Bertha and E. B. Ashton. *I Lift My Lamp: The Way of a Symbol.* Port Washington, New York: Ira J. Friedman, Inc., 1948.

Russell, John. "A Face That Really Launched 1,000 Ships—and Many More." *Smithsonian* 15, no. 4 (July 1984): 46–55.

Simon, Kate. "Saluting the Statue of Liberty." *Travel & Leisure* 14, no. 7 (July 1984): 78–85.

Trachlenberg, Marvin, *The Statue of Liberty.* New York: Viking, 1976.

Weinbaum, Paul. *Statue of Liberty, Heritage of America.* KC Publishers, 1979.

Willensky, Elliot. "A Nation Finally Remembers." *Historic Preservation* 35; no. 4 (July/August 1983): 14–19.

ABOUT THE AUTHOR

Mary Virginia Fox was born in Richmond, Virginia. She graduated from Northwestern University. Ms. Fox is the author of more than twenty books. She lives with her family in Middleton, Wisconsin.

974.7
F

Fox, Mary Virginia

The Statue of
Liberty

DATE DUE

BRODART		04/88	9.79
APR 2 3 1997			